PUSHES and PULLS

Anna Claybourne

This library edition published in 2016 by Quarto Library., an imprint of QEB Publishing, Inc.

6 Orchard, Lake Forest, CA 92630

© 2016 QEB Publishing,
Published by Quarto Library., an imprint of Quarto Publishing Group USA Inc.

Distributed in the United States and Canada by
Lerner Publisher Services
241 First Avenue North
Minneapolis, MN 55401 U.S.A.
www.lernerbooks.com

A CIP record for the book is available from the Library of Congress.

ISBN 978 1 60992 888 9

Printed in China

Publisher: Maxime Boucknooghe
Editorial Director: Victoria Garrard
Art Director: Miranda Snow
Series Editor: Claudia Martin
Series Designer: Bruce Marshall
Photographer: Michael Wicks
Illustrator: John Haslam
Consultant: Penny Johnson

Words in **bold** can be found in the glossary on page 22.

CONTENTS

3

On the move

Things around us are constantly moving. Birds fly through the air. Plants sway in the wind. Cars zoom along roads. Rain falls from clouds in the sky.

But what makes things move?

TRY THIS

Find a small ball or marble and place it on a table top.

◀ In some sports, such as soccer, the ball moves around all the time.

How many ways can you make the ball move?

Push it.

Flick it.

Blow it.

Can you make a marble change direction?

What happens if you do nothing to the ball?

Objects do not move on their own. They only start to move when something pushes or pulls them. These pushes and pulls are called **forces**.

Pushing and pulling

Push and pull forces can make toy cars move. Try this experiment with your friends.

TRY THIS

You need a car for each person. Make sure all the cars are about the same size.

1 Line up your cars somewhere with enough space, such as in a school hall or in a corridor.

2 After three, everyone must push their car as hard as they can.

Whose car goes fastest and farthest?

3 What happens if you stick two cars together? If you push the first car forward, the second car gets pulled along with it.

▲ Use tape to attach the front of one car to the back of another.

STRETCH AND SQUEEZE

Pushes and pulls can change things in other ways too. Squeezing modeling clay is a type of push. Stretching modeling clay is a type of pull. Squeezing and stretching change the shape of the clay.

Modeling clay

Stopping

Pushes and pulls don't just make things move, they make them change direction, slow down, speed up, and stop.

What would happen if you pushed your toy car into another, upturned car?

The upturned car makes your car stop with a force that pushes back. Although the other car is not moving, it still has a pushing force.

BANG!

TRY THIS

Roll a marble along the floor then try to stop it with different things, such as a book, a sheet of paper, and your hand.

Your hand?

A book?

A marble?

Which things stop the marble moving?

When the marble's way is blocked, you make a pushing force. If the force is strong enough, it pushes against the marble and stops it.

The pushing force of the paper is weaker than the pushing force of the moving marble. So the marble is not stopped.

A dangling strip of paper?

9

Dropping

If you hold an object at arm's length and then let go, what happens to it?

Most objects fall to the ground if you drop them. If you jump up, you fall back down, too.

Objects fall because they are being pulled. This pulling force is called **gravity**. It pulls things down toward the center of our **planet**, called Earth.

When you jump into the air, gravity pulls you back down.

Gravity in space is not as strong as on Earth. This is why astronauts appear to float around. They also find it easy to make high jumps and leaps!

Earth's gravity pulls things toward it. It pulls you down, so that you don't float away.

Getting faster

As an object falls or rolls downhill, it speeds up and goes faster and faster. This is because gravity pulls it downward.

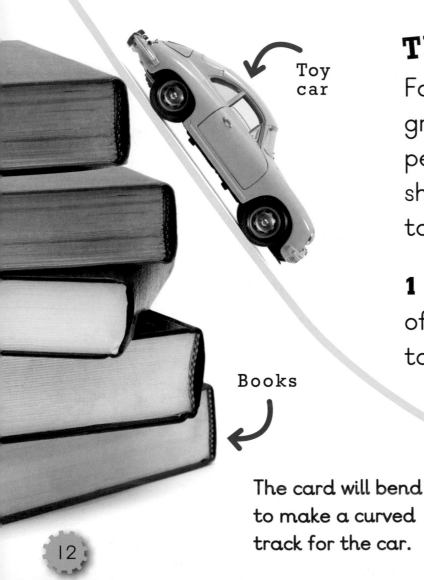

Toy car

Books

The card will bend to make a curved track for the car.

TRY THIS

For this experiment with gravity, you will need two people, a small toy car, a sheet of cardstock, sticky tape, and a few books.

1 Fix the card against a stac of books, using sticky tape, to make a steep slope.

Card

2 Hold the car at the top of the slope. Let it go and watch gravity pull it down to the bottom.

3 Ask a friend to let go of the car. Use your hand to stop the car near the top of the card.

4 Now try stopping the car near the bottom of the slope.

At the top, it is going slowly, so it hits your hand gently.

At the bottom, the car is going much faster, so it hits your hand harder. Ouch!

Skiers pick up speed as they zoom downhill. Gravity pulls the skier downward.

Slowing down

If you throw a ball, or push a toy car, it doesn't keep going forever. Eventually it will slow down and stop.

Try pushing a coin across a smooth surface, like a table.

Table top

The coin moves a little way after you push it. But it soon slows down and then stops.

The coin doesn't slow down by itself. A force called **friction** makes it stop. This happens when the coin rubs against the table as it slides.

Coin

Try to slide the coin
on different surfaces.
What happens?

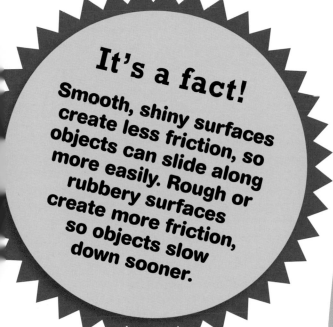

It's a fact!
Smooth, shiny surfaces
create less friction, so
objects can slide along
more easily. Rough or
rubbery surfaces
create more friction,
so objects slow
down sooner.

Rock climbing is easier in
rubber-soled sneakers,
because friction gives
them more grip.

ry pushing the coin across
metal tray and a carpet.
/hich has more friction?

Metal tray

Carpet

Useful friction

Friction can be very useful! It means the soles of your shoes and feet can grip the ground. Without friction, your feet would slide around and your hands would struggle to hold things.

TRY THIS

You will need a plastic bottle, water, cooking oil, and an adult to help you.

1 Fill the plastic bottle with water. It is heavier, but you can still pick it up.

2 Rub some oil on one hand. Now try to pick up the bottle with that hand. What happens?

It's a fact!

The oil makes it hard to grip the bottle, because oil has less friction than your hand.

When things rub against each other, friction produces heat.
This can be useful on a cold day because rubbing your skin warms it up.

Friction makes motorbike tires heat up and helps them grip the road surface.

Friction warms your hands when you rub them together.

▶ Rub a cold coin on a smooth floor. The friction will warm the coin up.

Pressure

Pressure happens when things press against each other. Air can be under pressure, as well as liquids and solids. The more air is squashed, the more it pushes back.

TRY THIS

A balloon holds air under pressure. Ask an adult to blow up a balloon and tie it to see how this works.

1 Gently squeeze the balloon. It pushes back against your hands.

The air in the balloon pushes back against your hand because the air is squashed in a small space under pressure.

2 Ask an adult to blow up another balloon, but leave it untied. Hold the end to keep the air in and then let it go. What happens?

The balloon zooms around the room. The air inside it pushes out of the open end. This moves the balloon along.

WATER PRESSURE

Water has a pushing force too. The deeper you go underwater, the more pressure is pushing on you.

Machines

Machines use forces in ways that help us in everyday life. Here's a simple machine you can make yourself.

TRY THIS

You need an eraser, a ruler, two yogurt containers, sticky tape, and four marbles.

1 Put the eraser on a table. Place a ruler on top of it, so that one end sticks out farther than the other.

Marbles

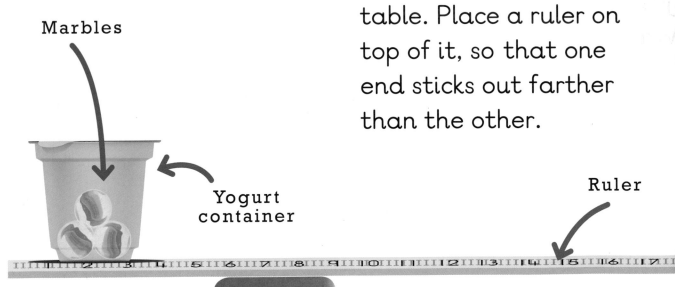

Yogurt container

Ruler

The balancing point, where the eraser is, is called the pivot.

2 Tape the two yogurt containers to either end of the ruler. Put three marbles in the container at the short end of the ruler. Put one marble in the container at the long end.

3 Now move the eraser under the ruler until it just balances horizontally. What do you notice?

It's a fact!
This type of machine is called a lever. It can increase the power of a force. Levers help to lift things. In our machine three marbles are lifted by the weight of one.

The single marble can lift three marbles in the air when it is farther away from the pivot.

GLOSSARY

Forces
Pushes and pulls that can make objects move, change speed, change direction, or change shape.

Friction
A rubbing force that can stop surfaces from moving against each other. Friction slows moving objects and produces heat.

Gravity
A pulling force that makes objects pull toward each other. The Earth's gravity pulls us down and stops us from floating off!

Lever
A simple machine that works by balancing a long stick on a point, called a "pivot".

Machine
An object that helps us do useful jobs by using forces.

Planet
A ball of rock and gases that circles around a star. We live on planet Earth that circles the Sun.

Pressure
A pushing force that happens when things press against each other.

22

INDEX

NEXT STEPS

- Encourage the children to spot forces in action in everyday life. For example, pushing a door to open it, or pulling a lid to open a box.

- Cars seem to move without being pushed or pulled. Discuss with the children how they move. The engine inside the car uses a fuel that push the wheels around.

- Ask the children to think of ways in which things that move are slowed down or stopped. Do some research to see how parachutes, car brakes, and train buffers work. Try making a parachute for a toy with the children and then testing it out.

- Gravity is working on us all the time. Discuss when we can feel it most, such as when our shopping bags pull down on our arms, and when we are pulled down to Earth when we jump.

- In space, gravity's pull is weaker than on Earth. Ask the children to discuss how they would do things in "zero gravity", such as hold objects down, stay in bed, or use the toilet. Why is gravity helpful? Ask the children to draw a picture of themselves in "zero gravity".

- Ask the children to look for objects that are made to have high friction. For example, the handle of sports equipment needs to have good grip and car tires need to grip the road.

- Look for different ways in which we use the pushing force of air or water and find out how they work. Examples could be a garden hose, a bicycle tire, and a vacuum cleaner.

- Look out for everyday examples of levers and discuss what we use them for. Seesaws and scissors are good examples of machines that work using levers.